The Healing
of A Culture

The Healing
of A Culture

Eugene Chiaverini

To order additional copies of this book, contact:
Xlibris Corporation
1-888-795-4274
www.Xlibris.com
Orders@Xlibris.com
73918

CONTENTS

ACKNOWLEDGEMENT

I would like to acknowledge those individuals who have played a meaningful role in my search for knowledge and understanding of the human mind, body and spirit and its connection to our creator.

I want to thank my family for their support through the good times and the difficult stressful events of life. They have always been my inspiration and source of happiness and peace. I want to thank all of the experts and wise sages throughout time whose wisdom, research and teachings have provided me the tools to evolve personally and professionally. Finally, I want to thank Amanda, Shawn and Terri for the time and energy they have invested in assisting me in organizing and editing the material in this book.

INTRODUCTION

The purpose of my first book, "Life Thoughts," was to look at my life experiences and choices and formulate some of the lessons that I have learned about myself and my spiritual journey and evolution. I reviewed the ethnic culture I grew up in, the time in history, and the impact that culture and time had on my development and maturation socially, religiously, morally, psychologically and spiritually. I examined the physical body and mind I live in and the impact it had on my self-concept, career choices, life choices, and learning style. I shared my three near death encounters and the impact they had on my spiritual beliefs and my ongoing studies in the areas of life force energy and my theory about life after death from this body. I explored my views on guardian angels, imaginary friends in childhood, the aging process and death, as we know it in our culture.

I discussed my views on why we are born, how our life missions are formulated and the concept of multiple life experiences in order to evolve as a soul. I had opportunities to make many choices that could have positive or negative outcomes. For every wrong turn, there was an opportunity to "right the course." Sometimes I did and sometimes I did not. In all instances, I was and am learning.

This interpretation is based on my spiritual belief system and the research I have invested in studying both Eastern and Western cultures and religions. These views work for me and my intention is simply to share them with others so they may benefit from my experiences and studying. I am not an expert in religion, metaphysics, science or history; however, I have found comfort and understanding in my interpretations of the meaning of life and cultures.

The lessons I learned were as follows:

* Understand how my brain and mind worked

* Be the teacher one moment and the student the next moment
* The power of positive thoughts
* What you think and practice is what you get
* You move in the direction of your most dominant thoughts
* Children need to have time to be children
* Children need to learn about boundaries, rules, and responsibility
* Parents must parent and teach children about boundaries, rules, and responsibility
* Schools and teachers need to be role models for children and set standards for behavior
* Teachers need to understand how each student learns and teach to that strength
* The concept of entitlement needs to be replaced with the concept of earned
* We need to go back to the concept of caring for others
* Family and roots are essential to understanding self
* Honesty and integrity need to replace self-absorption and greed
* We need to practice forgiveness to self and others
* We need to live our life with love and trust, not fear and doubt
* There is a life force greater than I am and I am part of that life force

This book focuses on the cycles of life in the individual, family and Nation, and how the stages of development, evolution or decay apply in all systems. The individual, family, and cultural have come into existence with dreams, goals, and needs. The how, when, and where those dreams, goals and needs get fulfilled, affect the development of each and its thinking, functioning and evolution. Let us now examine how the evolution and deterioration of each system impacts on the others and how we as a nation can right the course of deterioration.

CHAPTER ONE

Individual and Cultural Life Goals
and Missions—Daring to Dream

The human spirit is born with lessons to learn and messages to teach. How we fulfill these objectives, or if we fulfill them, is our choice. In life, we will have the opportunity to revisit these choices and choose again. If the same themes keep emerging and we do not explore them, we should take the time to sit still and ask ourselves—WHY?!

I remember a man who came to see me for counseling services regarding a consistent feeling of unsettledness and lack of fulfillment in his life. He was a successful lawyer and had a good marriage and family life, so what was happening? After months of sharing and exploring, he came to the realization that he had always had a dream of being a rabbi, but gave in to the family tradition of going to law school. His children were all grown and his financial needs and commitments were fewer. We explored the possibility of pursuing his dream and what this would mean to him. He set forth a plan to move in that direction with the support of his family and enrolled in a program for rabbinical studies. His mood and affect changed and he felt no further need to see me in counseling. Several years later he contacted me to announce that he was a Rabbi and that his depression had lifted and he felt a sense of fulfillment. He was doing God's work and used his legal training to assist him in parts of his work.

This is just one of many examples of how the human being has many paths in the journey of life to achieve their physical, mental and spiritual evolution. Through the process of sitting still, examining our inner voice and daring to talk about our inner thoughts we can open the door to resolution and growth. We never lose knowledge; we just forget how to tap it! In quiet moments of meditation or contemplation, I have often gone back to my childhood and replayed tapes of events, thoughts, and dreams that were clues to some of my goals or areas of growth that could be addressed in my life. However, as a child, I was consciously not aware of the message. It was just fun, play, or dreams. Later in life I was able to reflect on these reoccurring themes and see that intuitively I knew where I needed to go and what I needed to do.

Have you ever asked a child at age four what they want to be when they grow up? Then again, ask them at eight, thirteen, and twenty. Often the answers are very different and often it is not due to maturation but to resignation. The message that we often get from others is "you can't or should not do that;" I believe that we need to take time to listen to the inner messages that are always there for our review and direction. We should always "dare to dream." If you dare to dream, if you keep dreaming and doing and trying, then you will meet people who will say "yes you should dream," and you will start to believe that you can. This process of "what you think" becomes "what you get," and what you get is part of who you are, is the self-fulfilling prophecy. Ceilings are for houses, not people.

I remember when I was in middle school there was a young man who had some serious emotional and learning difficulties and was the victim of cruelty by other students. I was a well-liked child by my peers and was tempted to join my peers in laughing at this student. An inner voice would not allow me to do this, it felt wrong. Part of this came from my parents, but part came from my insides. I remember one day this young man was so hurt and frustrated that he went after some students with a pencil in his hand, like a weapon. I grabbed him and began to talk to him and he started to cry and we talked some more. We were 11 years old and we were talking about feelings. The event ended and a new event happened. Some of the students who were teasing him came over and invited him to join in the activities. I believe this had a positive impact on many levels, the victim may have learned something about trying to trust again and about his worth as a person. The other students might have learned about empathy and acceptance and I learned about the power of love and modeling.

Throughout the years of my work with youth and young adults, I have noted that a core obstacle, which emerges repeatedly, is the process of giving up on "what they can do." Children will come to see me as 12 year olds and be unable to tell me what they would wish to be when they grow up. If I pursue this with them and ask what they remember wanting to be when they were five or six, they could answer with many things. They would do what most children do; list a number of jobs from being an astronaut to being a racecar driver. Their faces would light up and we would laugh. I would then ask them what about at age nine and many would have just a few choices and by age 12 there were none. They would eventually talk about how they realized that they were not smart enough or strong enough or rich enough and on and on. Where did all of this stuff come from? Why did they give up on the dreams? In many instances, I learned that they gave up on those dreams because of adults passing on the message that it would never happen because of the reason mentioned above. Our world has become focused on selection by test results, grades, and skill levels at an early age. We have overlooked the individuality of maturation, determination, and learning style. We tend to pigeonhole children and not see the hidden gifts that each child possesses. If the child loses the confidence to be the best they can be, then the world has lost a contribution and a person has given up on a dream. Everyone loses . . . the individual, family, community, and culture.

There was a young man I saw years ago who was having difficulty learning in school. He was highly distractible, impulsive, and a poor reader. He was getting more and more uncontrollable in the classroom. He was placed in a school for learning disabled children and during the course of getting to understand this child, it was discovered that he had a hidden artistic gift. The staff worked with his strengths and helped him succeed in the classroom and excel in his artistic gifts. I lost contact with him after high school but one day got a note from him stating that he was an artist in New York and doing well in life. What a waste of a life had this child been left to be a square peg in a round hole!

The world is full of FLK's—funny looking kids. This coupled with different learning styles and maturational processes, sets the stage for possible trouble and victimization. How many FLK's grew up to be "not funny looking adults?" How many grew up to excel in certain areas and in adulthood had well respected achievements? A lesson learned is that every human being has strengths and we need to stop predicting and directing life journeys and choices to children. Allow individuals to flower at their own pace.

I remember when I was in elementary school having difficulty reading. I saw the words differently than they were written and sometimes they would move and I would lose my place. I also had trouble remembering my multiplication tables. This became a source of embarrassment to me and I would dread having to read aloud or go to the chalkboard to do math problems. This problem continued until I learned some techniques to compensate for my difficulties. I was a good musician, I could play many instruments without formal training, and I could learn to read music by hearing the notes in my ear and mind and then read the printed notes. Later, I learned that I was Dyslexic and that I was an auditory and kinesthetic learner. Once this became my learning method I was able to do well in college and graduate school. Some teachers in middle school would tell me to think about learning a trade and not consider college. Had I listened to them I would not have contributed to the world my knowledge and skills in counseling and human services. In fact, I would not have accomplished my dreams.

When I was a delegate to China in 2006, I became aware of the high number of suicides among Chinese adolescents. This was partly due to the fact that only one percent of the young adult population achieved admission to the higher education programs. This decision is made at the middle school years. These students are labeled as the less intelligent and must go to vocational programs or general labor work. For many young people life takes on a bleak and hopeless image. Many of these children thought that they had shamed their families and many choose death. Life without dreams can be depressing, bleak and hopeless. Are we making the same mistakes?

Growing up can be a difficult and emotionally turbulent process. Children are faced with competitiveness from early on. We enroll them in dance lessons, art classes, sports programs, music lessons, and advanced learning programs. This, in and of itself, is not bad as long as the motive or goal is socialization, recreation, and exploration. Much of this happens while children are attending Pre School centers. Years ago, children prior to the age of five or six learned how to socialize, play, and be happy. Then the world got more complicated and demanding. Families moved away from each other, both parents needed to work; single parent families increased in numbers and this country looked at the Far East and their educational process and systems. Our far eastern competitor's were outclassing us. So, the game began and the pressures increased. The theme was "Teach our children more and teach them at an earlier age and train our athletes at an earlier age," even before their bodies are ready. For those children whose minds and bodies marched to a timetable different from their peers, times got tougher.

Let us take some time to review the purpose, role, and maturation of the human being. The human brain is a marvelous creation, with cells and neural pathways that reach to and from every part of our body. The brain receives electrical impulses from these various regions and sorts them out, responds to them, and files them away for later use. If one part of the brain is injured other parts will often compensate—a more recent discovery by medical science. If certain areas of the brain are injured, especially during gestation or because of trauma, other parts seem to be intensified in their functioning. For example, if vision is impaired, then hearing or touch might be more sensitized. Thus, some individual may show more skill at drawing than reading. Many dyslexic children demonstrate enhanced skill at kinesthetic activities and many visually impaired individuals have a heighten sense of hearing music and producing that which they hear kinesthetically, such as playing it on an instrument or singing. The educational system needs to recognize how a child processes information, teach to the child's strengths, and assist the child in the development of compensatory skills, while encouraging the child to excel at learning. Children must understand that because they learn differently does not mean that they are less capable or less bright. All children have a gift or strength and it is up to the adults in that child's life to find them, recognize them, work with them and assist the child to succeed. Therefore, it is vital to understand that the processing of information in the human brain is important to modeling a successful and happy child. Labeling and segregating is NOT the answer. Just as parenting is hard work, so is teaching.

How did civilization survive all those past centuries? How did the great minds, artists, writers, scientist, architects, and inventors develop their gifts? History tells and shows us how the creative minds that left their mark on the world with their production of such gifts as The Seven Wonders of the World and great art with designs and images centuries ahead of their time. These great minds produced their insights and knowledge at times in their lives when they were ready to harvest their intellectual and creative gifts and concepts. Some were trained in other professions and later evolved into artist, inventors, healers, or authors. They were not all identified in childhood as possessing greatness in one certain area.

True, today, we live in a more sophisticated and complex world, but perhaps we have again "tossed out the baby with the bath water." Why have we become a society of directing and deciding rather than nurturing and allowing? What are the repercussions of such philosophies and actions?

There is the risk of lost dreams, lost hope, and lost gifts to our world, in addition to unfilled and wasted human potential. The effects of these actions have an impact on all systems; individual, family, culture, world, and the universe. I will refer to this in later chapters.

CHAPTER TWO

The Need to Be Perfect and to Have
Instant Gratification-The Quick Fix

The Family

Let us take a minute to examine a trend in our country to strive for instant gratification and physical perfection and the implications for our culture. In decades past, children were taught they had to earn things and that good things come to those who were patient. We were told that we were not the X or Y family. Sure, we were disappointed with that answer and sure, we had our little fuss . . . but the answer was still no and we survived. Most of the time, we eventually got what we asked for, if it was appropriate, and when we got it we were overjoyed. Sometimes we changed our mind and decided we really did not want it and sometimes we learned that our friends were no longer so cool and we were not friends anymore. We decided that it was not important to be like that individual.

We learn lessons from the word "no", such as patience, planning, self-control, humility, respect, appreciation, and how to cope with disappointments. When that "no" lesson is not learned in childhood our youth run the risk of growing into adulthood believing that they come first and foremost and have no responsibility or loyalties to others. They may grow up and become CEO's, politicians, teachers, and neighbors who have less hesitancy to break the laws, deceive their friends, family and associates, and lie for personal power and financial gain. We increase the potential to create an adult culture where substance, character, morality and honesty are less valued. More of our youth today live in a world of instant gratification, over exposed to adult behaviors and the inability to enjoy the wonders of being children. They grow up too fast and are not able, physically or intellectually, to deal with the consequences of adult decision-making. The biggest lesson you learn from "instant gratification" is that you are the center of the universe. Hmmm! Sound familiar?

In addition, many children in this country are stressed by the price they pay for social acceptance. We see pressure from media and peers to follow the cultural craze of what and how to dress. TV and movie stars, athletes, and entertainers are the role models for dress and behavior. They set the standards which are not always appropriate for children and young adults, and they often demonstrate "bad behavior." Often parents give into pressure by their children to purchase inappropriate clothing and to watch inappropriate TV shows and movies because "their friends do." Worst yet, they do not supervise their children's activities. The trend is to grow up quickly and be like "the stars," instead of being children. Children today have cell phones with cameras, which can lead to all kinds of inappropriate behaviors, and they have access to computer web sites that are not regulated strictly enough to prevent inappropriate activities, images and correspondence. These technical advances of this century are necessary; however, they have opened the door to all sorts of social and behavioral problems. Parents need to understand that children need rules and boundaries to protect them from poor decision-making skills. Let me repeat: there is a word that would work well to stem the tide of this trend and it is "NO". Parents may be afraid to say no because of the fear of their child being angry with them or not liking them, or the fear of hurting their child's self image. Saying "no" does not in itself ruin a child's self-image—other things play into that issue. Self-image has roots in success and the ability to have recognition of one's strengths in certain areas. Thinking good things about oneself and being encouraged to try new activities.

Another part of the self-image issue, that confronts many of our youth, is the concept of the "perfect weight." We see an alarming increase in eating disorders in young adults. Male and females are measuring their ability to be liked, successful or competitive based on their body size. They will purge food from their bodies, with addictive regularity, in order to achieve a magical size that ends up being thinner and thinner and causes physical danger to themselves. Sometimes this can cause permanent organ damage and can cause death. In other cases they will take steroids and other growth producing substances that will force their bodies to grow bigger and stronger, without considering the damage that these substances will do to their bodies and minds in later years. The message they get from their role models, the professional athlete, actors, and entertainers reinforces this trend.

I remember a young woman I saw in counseling who had a history of an eating disorder and later, as a young adult, began the process of addictive cosmetic surgery. No matter what she had done to herself, she always saw a flaw in herself. The flaw was really in her "mind's eye." She was to most standards a beautiful person on the outside, but on the inside she was damaged goods. Change had to occur from within.

All humans are born with a genetic history. What you do with that history, how you use your strengths, and how you take care of your body and mind will enable you to be successful in your life. You learn this by exploring and practicing and by being guided by adults. I have seldom met a child who would consistently move in the direction of failure if given the option of success, and guided through the process. The color of your hair, eyes and skin, body size and shape are all greatly determined by a genetic selection process. Today, many adults want to manipulate the genetic structure and control characteristics they want in their child, including gender. Some individuals in the medical profession and in research are supporting this trend. Adults say that they want to protect their child from the dangers of bad genetics; however this often has more to do with parental egos. I am in favor of the elimination of disease through genetic means, but I am not willing to push the envelope to other extremes. We need to have sound checks and balances in place, boundaries that keep us from drifting too far from sound practices. Go back to what I said earlier, that we are here to learn, grow, and evolve in our mind, body, and spirit, through life experiences and choices. The role of parents is to plant the seed, nurture it, protect it, guide it, and encourage it to explore and grow spiritually, physically, mentally, and emotionally. Parenting is hard work and requires consistent observation and intervention, mixed with love and encouragement. Parenting requires acceptance of their child. Behavior, appearance, and healthy habits can and should be molded and shaped so that a sense of right and wrong, good and bad, acceptable and unacceptable take hold and root. In essence, you help shape the child's moral, spiritual, and social values. Now the foundation for positive self-esteem and safe risk taking are set. The child is now prepared to make informed choices and deflect negative pressures. My experience and education tells me that the parents who want to use genetic manipulation to create the "perfect child" will not be satisfied with the finished, born product, because the real motivation rests in the parent's expectations and unfinished personal business about their own feelings growing up with hurt and disappointments. Much of this is about their own needs to be someone other than who they are, acted out through their child. Parents can practice good parenting and model for their child, or they can take short cuts, without hard work, and pass on that message to their children.

How well have you prepared the next generation to carry on the task of continuing the American Dream? Are you addicted to instant gratification? We need to correct the course we are following regarding perfection of body and refocus on mind and character. We need to focus on patience and earned rewards. Those are part of the values that has made this country historically strong and a model for other nations.

The Child and Expectations

The definition of expectation is a strong belief or hope that a particular event/action/reaction will happen. A mental image of something expected by or of somebody, or a standard of conduct or performance expected by someone. When does this concept of "expectation" set-in to our mental and intellectual process? How does this relate to the cause-effect factor? In infancy, the child learns that hunger produces a physical discomfort, which elicits a crying response, which prompts the adult to feed the child, which elicits comfort in the child. Both the child and the parent learn from this process and a set of expectations is established. Multiply this by a hundred thousand times per year of life and the stage can be set for life. Relief from discomfort is part of what the human desires and if this occurs with some degree of consistency then the world takes on the expectation of a safe, trusting, and loving place. If the early and ongoing responses are frustrating and even painful then the world becomes an unsafe and fearful place. Therefore, we need to learn that the world is safe and loving and we need to learn that our physical, social, and emotional self will be nurtured, and at the same time, all of our desires may not be instantly gratified. We need to learn patience, coping skills, planning, and delayed gratification in areas that are not life threatening. This process is what makes parenting "hard work" and thought provoking.

The question that needs to be asked by parents is, "what am I feeling at this moment and why?" Am I the parent/ teacher, or am I a child reacting to some inside fears, or needs from my own life past or present, or both? Is my expectation of a fearful world or a safe place? Is the situation that I am reacting to real or perceived? Is the real or actual effect of that situation as good or as bad as I expect it to be? As a parent, I personally, have either over reacted or under reacted to life situations that my children were experiencing, as if it were me experiencing it, and later discovered that my child was not experiencing it the same way. As a parent, you need to communicate with your child and find out how they are feeling. You need to help your child deal with their feelings and learn how to cope with both the good and bad of life events. You need to help them become problem solvers and feel confident in their ability to handle the vicissitudes of life. Most of all you need to be in touch with yourself so that you can avoid over or under reactions. You can then protect your child from danger and teach at the same time. As a child becomes comfortable with navigating the currents of life they will be able to apply those skills to adolescent and adult situations. Remember, parenting involves teaching, modeling, supporting, protecting, and preparing the child so that their expectations are realistic and accurate.

How these EXPECTATIONS evolve leads to a concept of ENTITLEMENT vs. EMPOWERMENT. Entitlement suggests that one is due or owed a certain outcome or opportunity. Empowerment suggests that one has the ability to travel a path, which leads to a certain outcome or opportunity. One word is synonymous with "given" and the other with "earned." We want our children to feel empowered, not believe they are entitled. Children who grow up with an internalized sense of empowerment become problem solvers. They understand the relationship of self and others. Children who grow up with an internalized sense of entitlement become takers, demanders and problem makers. They primarily desire self-gratification, even at the expense of others. Children who grow up with an internalized sense of empowerment understand the concept of earning the fruits of their labor. Children who grow up with the concept of entitlement are handed what they want without having to earn or work for anything. Think about how this influences learning, sports, socialization, employment, decision-making, politics, and relationships in a person's life! The expectations of each individual are molded by their perceptions of themselves and their world; such as trust, love and safety VS mistrust, fear and uncertainty, or morality and sense of right and wrong. It also impinges on the formation of character, such as a fractured character with gaps and flaws, and a desire for power and control.

Now, we must be careful in the process of providing the opportunity for self-realization to all individuals that we do not create a sense of entitlement. It is easy to create a monster while trying to save a soul. By this, I mean that in protecting an individual from pain and failure, one can create an unrealistic belief that all will be painless and forthcoming, without the ingredient of hard work and effort. In my work with children with special needs, I discovered that some well-intentioned parents took the advocacy role to a different plateau. They worked hard to ensure that their child was not left out of the learning process, or more importantly, exposed to pain and humiliation in the learning environment. Their goal was to make the world /school a safe place; however, they became watchdogs not advocates. Trust was replaced with distrust and the parents monitored the teachers and other students with super sensitivity. Some children learned that they could sidestep the action of hard work, which for many of them was "super hard work" and act out at home and at school. They learned how to expect special rules and exceptions in the learning process. Once this overreaction was recognized, all parties needed to regroup and develop a plan with trust, support, and consistency. The child could now realize that they were entitled the opportunity to learn and were empowered with skills to get the job done. Most importantly, they learned that once the playing field was level, they had to work hard to get the reward of success.

This very principle applies not only to school but also to life in general: socialization, sports, relationships, employment, parenting, and aging. What do you expect from your friends? What do you expect from a coach? What do you expect from your partner? What do you expect from your employer? What do you expect from your children? What do you expect from life? What do you expect from death? What do you expect from YOURSELF? How did this set of expectations develop? Are they real and appropriate, or feared and inappropriate? Do they get you what you want or impair your goal attainment? If they were not productive, would you change them?

Remember, "What you think consistently . . . is what you get." You move in the direction of your dominant thoughts. Take ownership, and be empowered to grow and change the outcome. The focus is on self, trust, concern for others, and an ingrained sense of right vs. wrong. This is then later reflected in the type of leadership we, as adults, elect on the local, state and federal level; the type of curriculum we choose in our schools; and the laws we legislate and support in our community, state and nation.

So how we prepare, and what we teach our children affects what they do as adults. This in turn, affects the following generation and the direction of the country. Each system has an impact on the other systems. Next we will examine how this is demonstrated in the evolution of America.

CHAPTER THREE

Life and Death of Great Societies

Morals, Values and Corruption

The history of all the great societies of the past teaches us that self-aggrandizement of the leadership, along with moral, ethical and spiritual decay eroded the sound principles of those cultures and eventually led to their destruction. Examine the societies that lasted hundreds of thousands of years, including our Native Americans. These were societies that began with concern for the welfare of not only the leaders, but for the citizens of that culture. Parents raised their children with a sense of a higher power; and, that their behavior on this planet had an impact on their life after physical death. There were rules for conduct, and consequences for those who violated those rules. There was an appreciation and respect for all life, and health and welfare programs for all citizens. Societies had a written code of conduct that was adhered to by all members of that culture and its leaders and government; serving as a constitution, of sorts, with rules and procedures, and laws and consequences for those who violated the rules.

As time passed, the people of those great societies, from leaders to ordinary citizens, developed moral and spiritual cancers. Focus moved from social values, self-integrity, morality and honesty, to personal gain economically, socially and politically, the need for instant gratification in all areas, and the insatiable need for power and control. Respect for each other gave way to mistrust of thy neighbor, relative and friend. The eventual outcome of this moral and spiritual decline was an economic and social collapse, the overthrow of the governing rules, and the death of that culture. The great lessons of life that were passed down from one generation to another were cast aside and replaced with self-absorption and personal gain.

Humankind needs to have boundaries and balance to stabilize growth and technical creativeness in all areas of life. We see this throughout adolescence, with the intense striving for acceptance, gratification, and exploration. As societies move through the stages of growth, from infancy to maturation, the same rules need to apply. If not, we run the risk of adolescent behavior at best, and corruption and decadence at its worst. Leaders who have not tasted the effects of a "time out chair," have difficulty with the concept of "no" and become very good at manipulating those around them to feed their own need for power and control at the expense of others and the good of the society.

The Birth of America and Testing its Values and Constitution

How and why was America founded? Our founding individuals and families were in search of a land where individuals could escape the corruption and persecution of the ruling class of their homelands. They were objects of class bias, religious persecution, and were denied freedom of speech and democratic representation in government and law. They left bondage for the promise of freedom. They sought a land where moral values were upheld and families had the right to educate their children academically and spiritually according to their beliefs. Colonies were established where people of similar philosophies gathered together to organize communities to practice and protect those values. Eventually these colonies joined together and drafted a constitution that protected their life, liberty and pursuit of happiness. This became the American Dream. Through war they won their independence from England and became a separate nation, The United States of America, and the birth of a new concept and a new way of life. As time passed, this country strayed from the objectives of their quest for freedom by imposing the same persecutions and bias on the original occupants of this land: the Native American. How quickly we forgot the lessons we had learned.

Over the centuries this great country of ours has experienced the testing of its constitution and the challenging of its resolve to have the individuals' rights protected by law. The concept of separation of local, state and federal government and the freedom of religious expression has been maintained and the checks and balances of power has been insured with the three separate branches of our government—legislative, judicial, and executive. Each individual had the opportunity to pursue his or her dreams and entrepreneurship thrived. Immigrants found refuge in our borders by way of laws that allowed their immigration and protected their status and eventual citizenship. We fought a civil war to correct injustices and preserve freedom for all. We fought World Wars to do the same. As a Nation, we moved from our infancy, through our preteens and into our adolescence. For the most part our country was a safe place and our constitution provided the format and the structure, like a family, to guide us and teach us right from wrong, good from bad, morality and spirituality, and consequences for bad behavior.

This country experienced economic and moral difficulties, from within, during the 1920's and 1930's and came close to deterioration morally, economically and socially; but the wisdom of the writers of the constitution and the structure of the government, kept the balance of power from escalating out of control and solutions were found. The fear of destruction of WWII regenerated this country's resolve and Americans regrouped and overcame the dangers of the time. The opportunity for each individual to reach their dream was reestablished and life in this land refocused on peace and prosperity. Historical themes and patterns used to regroup in troubled times reflected the following process:

* Hopes and dreams
* Prosperity
* A tendency to disregard old values
* National or World crisis
* Crisis resolution and refocusing on the values that held America together; country, family, hope, community, spirituality, honesty and integrity

Most individuals were raised with a sense of right verses wrong and the consequences of wrong. We were, in general, a moral culture. There was always an understanding of the words "no" and "stop" and these words applied to all citizens. Those who chose to ignore these words faced the consequences of such actions. Now there were some who circumvented the laws and got away with it, but most didn't. Injustices were recognized and actions were taken to correct them. At times the progress was slow; however, in the end, patience, perseverance and action resolved many injustices. We were still an adolescent culture and we needed to reestablish boundaries to keep us from social, moral, and spiritual corruption.

Then, in the 1960's, the adolescent behavior of America pushed the boundaries and the nation became complacent in the use of the "time out chair" socially, politically, spiritually and in the family. It was a time when many changes needed to occur in order for our country to further the process of correcting racial, ethnic, social, and gender inequalities and the pursuit of our constitution which guarantees the rights of all the people to pursue their dreams. However, change needs to be guided with clear goals and a sound process. Like adolescents, there is the danger of expanding the objectives, pushing the envelope and seeking instant gratification and pushing aside impulse control. Allow the teenager to stay out to eleven and they will try for midnight.

The many needed social changes did begin to take place during this time of awareness; however, we moved beyond the stated goals and objectives and got swept up in the current of impulsive and counterproductive behaviors. With fewer checks and balances on the process, we rushed into an era of social, ethical and moral decay. The concept of empowerment was mixed up with entitlement. Established political, social, spiritual and family philosophies and values were overshadowed by a push for "new age" thinking. In attempting to save the culture we created cancers, which began to grow untreated. "No" was replaced with "try to stop me." Time out chairs were replaced with litigation and lawsuits by the wrongdoers. Consequences for bad behavior were challenged or overlooked. The individual's needs overshadowed the greater needs of the culture. Self-aggrandizement and a sense of me first became acceptable. Boundaries became blurred and the foundations on which this country was established were being challenged. Recreational drug use was becoming an acceptable practice; sexual morays were being tossed aside; religious beliefs were challenged and schools were stripped of their authority to teach their curriculum or discipline students without fear of lawsuits. Teachers within our school felt free to cross the sexual boundaries with students. Youth gangs became family surrogates for youth. We were becoming a violent, drug using, self-centered country.

As the twenty first century began its first nine years, the structure and foundation of America was continuing to crack and decay. The continued decay is reflected in the following manners:

* Children continue to be exposed to adult behaviors via the Internet, television, unsupervised free time, and advertisements. The age of childhood innocence is disappearing.
* Schools are being challenged in courts for enforcing rules and regulations regarding behavior of students, dress codes, and academic standards.
* Teachers are forced to teach a curriculum devoid of spiritual believes and moral values. The teaching of history, government, and civics is often distorted and misrepresented.
* Gangs are operating within the school environment of most middle schools and high schools.
* Academic standards in many schools have dropped.
* Sexual behaviors in the schools have increased on all levels.
* STD's and pregnancies in both high school and middle school have increased.
* Many parents spend less time parenting, instead of using their time constructively and balanced. It is not quantity but quality of time that counts.
* The concept of "cause and effect" for bad behavior in school has been replaced with favors promised if a child was good, bribing the child, and threats to administrators by parents if disciplinary actions are initiated.
* Instant gratification is replacing earned reward.
* A "me first" generation is growing as a national philosophy.
* Children are growing into adulthood internalizing the unhealthy philosophies and values they learned in childhood.
* Financial and personal gains are replacing spiritual and family values.
* The concept of entitlement is replacing the concept of earned.
* The fast-track to success is replacing hard work and good character.
* The belief in a higher power is being ridiculed.
* Greed, corruption and dishonesty have permeated all levels of society educationally, socially, politically, religiously and economically.
* The economic stability of America has weakened and is approaching a collapse.
* The dreams of retired citizens are threatened by actual or feared loss of income and healthcare in their senior years.
* This nation is being flooded with personal, family, social, financial, spiritual, political and moral bankruptcy.

CHAPTER FOUR

The Healing Process

History, not forgotten, is the teacher of things to come

How can we, as Americans, treat this cancer within our society? What are the tasks that must be taken to treat this illness and stop our cultural decay? We have learned from science that one must treat the cause, not just the symptom. If you just treat the symptom, another symptom will appear in its place. We also know that infection in one area spreads and infects another area. In human behavior and ethical pathology the same principle applies. We must heal on all levels and in all systems from the inside out.

First and foremost, we must go back to the principles, goals and objectives that made this country great. The roadmap rests within our constitution and bill of rights, and our belief, as a nation, that there is a higher power than self. They rest within the dreams of our founding fathers and the reasons they came to these shores. They came for religious and spiritual freedom and the promise of the right to openly practice those beliefs in their family, churches, community and country. They came for the right to be self governed by elected officials who represented these philosophies and who would strive to preserve the constitution and bill of rights. They worked hard to establish the three separate branches of government that brought about the checks and balances to avoid dictatorship and abuse of power. We need to take a look at the current trend of sidestepping and/or trying to eliminate that structure. We need to reestablish the boundaries and the process that made us a strong governing nation and a model for the free world.

Next we need to "clean up our act" on all levels. Honor, morality, respect for each individual's life, liberty and the pursuit of happiness. This must start at five levels, the individual and family unit, educational system, community, government and the judicial system.

In the family, parents need to encourage their children to be children and enforce rules that teach love, respect, morals, spiritual/religious beliefs, patience, hard work, boundaries, honesty and integrity. Parents need to teach children the fact that bad behavior has consequences and how to deal with those consequences. In essence, parents need to go back to the tough business of parenting. These young citizens can then have an opportunity to grow up to be responsible adults who can better uphold the values of this country, enforce the laws, and carry out the political process needed to maintain the rights of all citizens. Our children need to relearn the concepts of respect for self and others, and forgiveness; and they need to replace the concept of entitlement with empowerment.

We must staff our schools with teachers who will do more than teach basic subject matter. They must be empowered to set standards for school and classroom behavior without fear of lawsuits and they must be empowered to teach American values as outlined in our constitution and bill of rights. We also must insist that teacher behaviors do the same and that the boundaries that separate teachers from students be maintained. This means that all teachers hired must have the moral character to not cross the lines in their verbal or behavioral actions.

The school administration needs to institute procedures to protect all students from gang behaviors, and eliminate the threat from students who have gang affiliations or participate in gang related activities within the school environment. Sexual behaviors and actions must be eliminated in the school environment and all students must be in supervised areas while in the school. Appropriate dress codes must be established and enforced for both faculty and students. All parents should sign a pledge form agreeing to support the school rules and regulations. All parents should also have the option to choose a school for their child that reflects their values and beliefs. Children must be allowed to live in a children's world void of adult distractions. And adults must model good behavior for their children. Out of control behavior such as behavioral misconduct, violence, and disrespectfulness must not be tolerated. The educational community needs to be a safe place for children to explore their dreams, learn about their strengths, and understand how they, as an individual, learn. Children must be encouraged to dream.

We, as a Nation, need to reevaluate our priorities. We have become a nation of addictions, such as power, money, instant gratification, self-centeredness and a sense of entitlement. This country needs to refocus on honesty, hard work, integrity, concern for others, and trust. We need to institute consequences for our elected officials who demonstrate dishonest behaviors, a sense of entitlement, selfishness, and greed. We need to brush off the "time out chair." Each individual and our elected government officials need to ask the tough questions about how much a person's time and skills are realistically worth. Is an educator worth much less than an actor or athlete? Should CEO's be more valuable than shop owners? Why have we rewarded them for unethical behaviors? Have we given them permission to be unethical and dishonest by our passive involvement in their business practices? Who else profited from this process? Is all productive work valuable in a free enterprise system and a society made up of all varieties, sizes, colors and beliefs of its citizens? What kind of role models have we glorified?

All adults need to work hard to become honest and ethical and to elect local, state and federal officials who uphold these values and demonstrate through their own actions the moral character that reflects honesty, integrity, respect for the laws of the land and the rights of all its citizens. These elected or appointed officials must believe and demonstrate the concept that the good of the country and its citizens takes precedence over personal financial gain and power.

Additional Methods of Healing the Mind and Body

We, as a people of this nation, must begin to heal from within. Throughout the history of humankind, music and sounds have played an important role in prayer and healing. The early-recorded histories of civilizations have left us pictorial or written illustrations of sounds and vibrations role in worship, medicine, and social and emotional well-being. This coupled with art and dance seemed to be essential tools in assisting the culture in its quest for answers and outcomes. WHY?

Modern science and research has given us some clues and in some cases, answers to the why. Plato and Shakespeare sought to find out the reason sounds and words had an effect on ones mood. Eastern religions combined sounds, smells and herbs to affect an individual's physical and emotional well-being. However, it was not until recent times that some measurable scientific evidence is starting to surface. Scientists, medical doctors, physicists, psychologists and other professionals are now spending time and money looking at and measuring the outcomes of these practices on the human mind, body, and spirit. Dr Michael F. Roizen, the Chief Wellness Officer of the Wellness Institute at the Cleveland Clinic, stated, "Listening to finer music and attending concerts on a consistent basis makes your real age about four years younger. Whether that's due to stress relief or other properties, we see decreases in all-cause mortality, reflecting slower aging of arteries as well as cancer-related and environmental factors."[1]

Another expert is Vera Brandes, the Director of the research program in music and medicine at the Paracelsus Private Medical University in Salzburg, Austria. Ms Brandes has worked with the University to research the effects certain music has on moods, illness healing and wellness. She has developed a music treatment program that works in cooperation with the patient's medical doctor, who establishes a diagnosis. The individual is sent home with a listening protocol and music loaded into a player system. The music tracks consist of original material developed by Ms. Brandes and her team. She has specialized in the treatment of psychosomatic illnesses, pain management, anxiety, depression, and insomnia.[2]

Dr. Masaru Emoto, Doctor of Alternative Medicine, has conducted research and published several books focusing on music and images to restore physical and emotional well-being. In his book, *Water Crystal Healing: Music and Images to Restore Your Well-Being,* he explains how healing music soothes the mind and body, and can correct distorted electrical frequencies within our cells. This leads to decreased joint and back pain, improved function of the nervous, circulatory, lymphatic, and immunes systems.[3]

The Kennedy—Krieger Cancer and Wellness Center and the Cancer Treatment Centers of America have incorporated a combined treatment modality approach to the treatment of patients who are admitted for cancer diagnosis and treatment. This approach includes prayer, meditation, music, diet, group support and traditional medical treatments. Many other teaching hospitals are also using similar programs in the care and treatment of patients with chronic illnesses, trauma recovery and post surgical healing. Ancient cultures practiced body movement to open up the flow of energy throughout our body. These cultures believed that illness was caused by blockages in our various energy centers called chakras. The use of body manipulation and configuration along with chanting and visualization would open the flow of energy throughout the body and restore health, both physically and emotionally.

If we combine all the tools and processes, past and present, study their impact on the healing of the body and the expansion of the mind, we can improve the quality of our life and the understanding of our life missions.

Life in our culture is full of traumatic events, some big and some small. Each of these events can have an impact on the functioning of our mind, body and spirit. Our physical self is made up of water, cells, neurons, chemicals, protein, electromagnetic energy, and so forth. We have various organs that regulate our body temperature and perform functions that keep use alive and thinking, growing, moving, breathing, seeing, smelling, tasting, feeling, fighting illness, and many other tasks. Research has demonstrated that humans have a positive and negative pole, an electromagnetic field, neurons, and protons like our planet and other matter in the universe. There is a common core to all life and energy in the universe. Science also tells us that electrical energy never simply disappears. It goes somewhere when it leaves its host environment.

We come from the universe, which some religions call Heaven and when we pass on, we return to the universe. When there is a trauma in the universe, it is felt by other objects in the universe and has an effect on the energy activity, from major impacts to minor ones. When there is trauma, on our planet, the same process occurs; and when we experience trauma in our lives, the effects are the same. The universe and planet, and mind, body and spirit can be impacted in either a positive or a negative way.

Let me now share some personal events in my life that have been traumatic and the impact they had on my mind, body and spirit. When I was a baby I developed, sever ear infections and pneumonia along with a high fever. Now, the specifics of this event are somewhat unclear because it was in 1940 and my parents have been deceased for twenty plus years. My mother did relay that a priest did give the last rights, so I must have been very ill. I survived and the impact of that trauma showed itself when I started school. I had difficulty learning to read. When I was in college, I was finally diagnosed as having a reading disorder and dyslexia. I was taught how to compensate for these issues and went on to have a very successful undergraduate and graduate experience. The trauma was an illness, which affected neurological processes in my brain and visual system.

A secondary impact was in my mind and spirit. In school, I began to doubt my ability to learn and compete with my peers. I did not recognize my power as a learner until I was in college. Fortunately, I learned strategies to compensate in high school and had other areas of strength to offset the reading problems and boost my self-esteem. There was a trauma, an impact, and a need to understand the trauma and the impact of the event on my person. (Event—Awareness—Understanding-Resolution)

Later in my adult life, I was showing symptoms of a lung disorder. It was discovered during a stress test at my doctor's office. I was having night's sweats, shortness of breath, and fatigue. I was hospitalized, and eventually diagnosed with Sarcoidosis, an inflammatory disease that, in my case, settled in my lungs. My lung dysfunction was so severe that the prognosis was poor. I had a family of seven children and I was only forty-two years old. Thus, the trauma was not only physical, but also emotional. I was treated for two years with steroids, which further complicated both my mind and body functions. The Sarcoidosis was suppressed but the affects of the steroids lingered. Mood shifts, weight gain, and necrosis in my hip, which was already at risk from a genetic feature passed on to me from my mother's side of the family.

Prior to this trauma, I was already involved in the study of power of life energy and the positive impact of meditation and prayer on healing of the mind, body, and spirit. I used this approach along with medication, to get well. I also used this time to intensify my study and understanding of what my life was all about. What was I suppose to do and learn while living? What was unfinished business? Through this process, I learned that there was much work to be done in the areas of personal growth, humanitarian work, and spiritual evolution. I became more aware of the direction I needed to go with my life.

In 2001, I had another trauma/near death experience. I was awakened at about midnight with a tightening feeling in my chest, as if a large boa constrictor was squeezing it. I was taken to the hospital and after checking into the emergency room, I went into cardiac arrest. I had to be defibrillated three times before my heart started to pump again. Later, I had bypass surgery. During this time, I experienced the following thoughts and images. I felt my body lifting off the gurney and moving upward toward a light at the end of a tunnel. I felt an insight that said I was ok and that I needed to finish my work in this life. I reinforced my belief that my life force was everlasting and part of a greater life force. I then felt myself going back to the gurney and I opened my eyes. From that moment on, I had a greater conviction and understanding of my spiritual self in relation to my physical self. Again, I rededicated myself to work on my mind/body/spirit evolution and to continue my work of teaching others about this process.

Two years later, I was riding my motorcycle when I was run over by an eighteen wheel steel truck. As I was under the truck, the back wheels were coming straight for my head. I asked God to be with me and the wheels scraped the top of my helmet and missed my head. I suffered eleven fractures to my ribs, backbone, and femur. Later I had hip replacement surgery, which was partly the result of genetics, steroids, and the truck accident.

I learned from my traumatic experiences the following:

* We were born to fulfill certain missions in life that enhance our evolution of mind/body/spirit and each event gives us the opportunity to become more aware and evolve.
* Each traumatic event has an impact on others around us.
* Our life force energy is one with a greater power in the universe and that the events in one time /space have an impact on all the others.
* Meditation, visualization, prayer, and sounds can facilitate the healing process of the body, as well as the mind.
* All parts of life integrate into the healing and evolutionary process.
* We need to avoid the "one size fits all" approach to healing.
* Individual health in mind, body and spirit impacts family, work, political values, community, the nation and the world.
* We each have things to do in our life—lessons to learn and lessons to teach.
* We have opportunities to finish unfinished business and have an impact on all life.

Healing the Spirit

God   YHWH   Allah   Bhagwan

* All life in the Universe begins with a thought from the creator, followed by action, production/creation, evolution, transition, trauma, reaction, relocation, and recreation.

    *   Nothing happens by pure chance. All life has energy that connects us together from the smallest particle to the vast solar system to the Universe and infinity. This process happens over and over again.

    *   There are many roads to achieve spiritual evolution and no one institution has ownership.

    *   The story has been told that Ghandi once said that in his heart he was Muslin, Buddhist, Hindu, Christian and Jew. He was assassinated because he would not proclaim that Muslims were more entitled than Hindus.

Since the beginning of recorded history, humans have worshipped a power or force greater than self. This creator entity has taken on many shapes and forms and many ideologies, yet each shares a similar set of rules for living that guide each culture spiritually, socially, ethically, morally, politically and educationally. The cultures that implemented those standards in their families, communities, education systems, and government thrived and lasted longer. Once there was the erosion of those values, the culture began a downward spiral and eventually was destroyed, either by outside forces or from within, due to corruption, greed, violence and immorality on all levels. Great texts were written outlining these rules of belief and conduct for humans. They each had different names and were produced at different historical times, yet, each has similar rules and guidelines for humankind and his/her beliefs, behavior, and evolution. They are the Koran/Qur'an, Torah, Bible, and Bhagavad Gita.

They speak of a greater force than humans. A force that is universal and is founded on the principles of love, forgiveness, morality, honesty, trust, family and a life after death from this earthly existence. Each views humans as imperfect creations with a major goal in life—that of the spiritual self-evolution of each soul. They each speak of Angels, Satan, Heaven, Hell, and some form of out of body self or energy. They each talk of the individual's free will. There were other cultures in history that also had written or drawn spiritual beliefs with similar themes, including the Native Americans.

Hinduism refers to the supreme creator as Bhagwan, Ishvara, Mahesvara, Para Meshvara. Sikhism refers to the supreme creator as Waheguru and Nirankor. Judaism refers to it as YHWH, Yahweh, Adonai, Hashem, and Elohim. Christianity refers to him as Yahweh, Jahova, and God. Islam refers to him as Allah. Bahai refers to it as Baha, Al-Abha. The Shangdi religion refers to the deity as Hanyu Pinyin.

The cultures that survived and evolved spiritually and morally also grew and evolved intellectually, socially, scientifically, economically, artistically, culturally, and emotionally. However, ingrained in each major religion over centuries, is a philosophy that proclaims ownership of God and declared the others as evil conspirators. Where did this ownership come from? It was not written in any of these books. Holy wars have been fought for centuries over this issue. In addition, as each religion grew in numbers, land ownership, economic gains and political power factor into the equation. Trust, love, charity, truth, peace, and harmony were replaced with mistrust, hatred, fear, possessiveness, aggression and violence—values which are inconsistent with the written text of each culture's "Holy Book."

How and Why did man's faith and spirituality, based on love, morality, nonviolence, honesty and compassion, continually move in the direction of war, rivalry with each other, persecution, corruption, power, and control and decay? How did a universal God become a sole possession of one belief system? Why would a loving creator establish a pecking order of favoritism among his creations? It sounds like children claiming that mom or dad loves them better than the other children. Why did humans fail to learn the lessons of their spiritual teachings? Why did they fail to see the relationship between spiritual decay and cultural, moral and social decay? Perhaps the truth is that power, politically, economically and scientifically, within each organized religion opened the door to corruption, immorality, dishonesty and war. Humans still have a long path to travel on their way to a higher level of spiritual evolution.

In America we see a similar spiritual pattern. Our earliest settlers came to these lands to escape religious persecution. There was a mixture of Catholics, Protestants and Native Americans. The Catholic and Protestant groups viewed the Native American spiritual practices as barbaric and evil, and they set out to convert them to Christianity to "save their souls." With that action they set into motion the same process of religious intolerance from which they fled. Christians believed that they had a special place with God and sole deed to God's graces. They were the favorite "child" of God. Understanding little about the history of the Native American spiritual roots and it's similarity to other ancient systems, and not having the benefit of modern day knowledge about life in the universe and modern science, and archeological findings of other holy books, they systematically eliminated the public practice of that culture's religion.

As time passed and America became a nation, the foundation of Christianity served as a compass for the constitution of this country and for the elected officials, as well as a roadmap for the laws of the land. Statements such as, "In God we trust" and "God Bless America," gave credence to our spiritual beliefs and our moral convictions. We celebrated holidays, prayed in schools, and taught courses about the history of Christianity. We also taught the history of other faiths and allowed our teachers to honor those holidays during school hours. At the same time we welcomed immigrants of other faiths and allowed them the freedom to practice their faith as long as it did not infringe upon the constitutional structure of our government. However, there continued to be an underlying belief that Christianity was the true faith and that other faiths needed to be converted.

During the later part of the twentieth century there began a movement to challenge the public expression of religion from public institutions, laws, holidays, school curriculum, workplace, advertisement, parks, and currency. The American Civil Liberties Union spearheaded the thrust to widen the legal parameters of "Separation of Church and State." They moved into the arena of challenging the very core of the founding fathers philosophy and the constitution of this country. In an attempt to level the playing field and protect the rights of all citizens they crossed the boundaries of the fair and balanced rights of all. They moved into questioning the curriculum taught, and the freedom of expression for all citizens.

With the advent of the twenty first century this population was challenging the right to believe in a God and to express it openly in advertising, on our currency, in our pledge to our flag and in our customs. The spiritual base of our country was and is being challenged. It is fascinating that this is coming at a time when the morality of our country is spiraling out of control. Corruption in our corporations, in our political system and officials, violence in our schools, scandals within our churches, bad behaviors from our role models and addictions within our communities. This is an overt display of greed, self-centeredness, and lust for power and wealth.

The values that made this country strong have been set aside and now we, as a nation, are becoming weak. History is being repeated and we have disputed the value of that history. In fact, we are not even teaching it or discussing it.

In our schools, administrators are supporting and encouraging the teaching of questionable moral, social, sexual and political subject matter and eliminating the value of teaching about God and religion. This is starting in the elementary school grades. We need to make sure that our schools are teaching subject matter that support the students' spiritual development and assist the student in viewing life as part of an evolution of mind, body and spirit. Self-aggrandizement and self-centeredness leads to a sense of entitlement and poor character development and a tendency to disbelieve in a higher power than self. Look at the track record of societies who were pro "Godlessness" and banded the expression of a spiritual belief. We need to examine those cultures, past and present, whose leaders saw them as the savior of their people, instead of a servant of their people. If you examine history you will come to the conclusion that we are traveling down a dangerous path that has historically had disastrous outcomes.

Cultures that are spiritually and morally sound develop citizens that are also morally sound. This, in turn, develops a formula for growth and evolution and the treatment of moral cancers. The culture that has strong individuals, who believe in God, regardless of religious affiliation, has the greatest chance of growth and evolution. This will lead to healing in all the other areas mentioned in this book. We need to go back to basics and the blending of what made this country strong. As my mother would say to those who asked her how she made her wonderful meals, "a pinch of this and dash of that and keep tasting it until its right." Never did she throw out the recipe.

CHAPTER FIVE

The Ingredients

The Recipe

In order for this great culture to strengthen its chance for survival, we need to adhere to the following list of ingredients:

* Every citizen of this great nation should read our Constitution.
* Parents need to plant and shape moral, spiritual and behavioral values in their children such as love, trust and kindness.
* Parents need to assist their children in valuing their individual strengths and dreams.
* Children need to feel empowered to work hard to achieve their dreams, not feel entitled to it.
* Parents need to be aware of the need for parenting their children—there is no substitution for this ingredient.
* Parents need to raise their children with a sense of a greater power than themselves.
* Children need to nurture their minds, bodies and spirit.
* The nation must not support addictive behaviors and the themes of instant gratification.
* Schools must be a safe place for our children to learn.
* Teachers must have the skills and moral integrity to teach our children.
* Teach our children about the teachings in the great books of the various religions and their common messages regarding life.

* Schools must teach both modern technology and core subjects so all students have both an understanding of the history of this country and the constitution which has preserved it and the knowledge of modern science and technology.
* We must use new and old technology together to achieve the proper objectives.
* Every elected official must be held to abiding by the constitution of this country.
* We must return to the foundations of our founding fathers dreams of life, liberty, freedom of speech and religion.
* Every individual needs to be held responsible for his or her actions and decisions.
* We must hold role models, elected officials, corporate executives, and religious leaders publicly accountable for their values, honesty and behavior and knowledge of our Constitution.
* Each individual should insist that words and promises be followed by appropriate and promised actions.

This recipe must be tasted regularly for the proper balance of its ingredients and adjusted if there are missing or forgotten parts or a need for adjustment of the amount. As with all great recipes, the test of taste, time, and blending ensures its survival.

Crossing with Honor—the last Ingredient

When I was preparing for a major living relocation after my retirement, I was confronted with the task of going through the all the stuff I had collected materially, intellectually and spiritually. I had the opportunity to brush off the memories and the dances that were attached to them. Each object or thought triggered a vision of the time and where in my own evolution I was coming from and moving towards. Before long I was creating a dance of my life, molded and shaped into different acts and chapters. I realized that this history should be passed on to my family so that they may have, if they choose, the opportunity to learn from my life lessons.

This process, which was initiated from within me, has been historically, a task that great cultures of the past have bestowed upon the elders of their communities. They were seen as the spiritually, experientially and intellectually wise. They were the teachers of the young, the role models for the youth and the consultants for the governing councils, the parent trainers and midwives, and the healers. They not only passed on the history of their culture, but also morals, values, pride, expectations, and rules of life. Life lessons were essential in avoiding the pitfalls of impulsive behaviors, corruption, greed, self-centeredness, and personal power earmarked for selfish reasons. These elder citizens were cared, for and about, in their golden years and valued for their contributions to their communities. In their most vulnerable time of life, they were protected and given dignity and respect. The full circle of life was ended as it began.

The value of the senior's life's worth of knowledge and contributions has changed over the past fifty years, not only in this country but globally. In 2006, I was fortunate enough to be part of a delegation that was invited to visit China and share human service concerns with the Chinese caregivers, organizations, and government officials. One of the difficulties they were facing was the care of the senior population in the urban and rural areas. Many seniors were being neglected physically, emotionally and medically, and many were isolated from their families. Their adult children both work, and the single child per family limits the amount of care given to this population by family members. Many families who were historically farmers have been relocated to cities because of massive rural projects to decontaminate rivers and build industrial complexes. Seniors were not only taken from their employment, farming, but also removed from their social ties.

The growing numbers of this population has strained the care giving system and the country has difficulty feeding, housing and providing medical care to them. These individuals historically were the most respected of their community. No longer is that the reality of today's world in China.

Today in the United States there is an alarming movement and a disturbing attitude emerging regarding our senior citizen population. I recently listened to a group of young college students speak about how upset they were at the thought of older retired persons making them have to pay for their social security "welfare checks" in the future. They seemed unaware of the fact that these senior citizens had paid portions of their paycheck into the system to pay for their income when they were too old to work. It was their income insurance policy. They appeared unaware of the fact that government had created a growing deficit in the social security funds through the misappropriation of these funds. In essence, the government had taken money out of the retirement bank accounts and spent it in other areas to solve financial problems in other programs.

It appeared that these young adults equated social security with public welfare. How and why were these individuals so misinformed? How did they get so self-centered that they would entertain the concept of taking from the elderly in order to give to themselves?

In addition, there is legislation pending that would limit the amount and quality of medical care available to senior citizens.

Are we at a point in our culture where we believe that the quality of life of the elderly is worth less than others? Are we as a nation disregarding the value of life and its lessons and the valuable knowledge each of these individuals has to share and teach the culture? We owe nothing less to our elderly than the opportunity to grow old with peace, dignity, care, and self-respect. They should be given the right and opportunity to cross over to the other side as they were born into life on this planet earth.

We need to open our eyes and minds to the facts of what is happening by our omissions and habits and take responsibility for righting the course of history. We need to continue to taste the ingredients that made this country a beacon of hope for the oppressed people of the world, before it is too late!

REFERENCES

1. Gurewitsch, Matthew, "Composing Concertos in the Key of Rx," *The New York Times,* March 25, 2009

2. Gurewitsch, Matthew, "Composing Concertos in the Key of Rx"

3. Emoto, Dr. Masaru, *Water Crystal Healing: Music and Images to Restore Your Well-Being,* Atria (October 17, 2006)

CHAPTER SIX

THE
CONSTITUTION
of the United States

We the People of the United States

We the People of the United States, in Order to form a
more perfect Union, establish Justice, insure domestic
Tranquility, provide for the common defence, promote
the general Welfare, and secure the Blessings of Liberty to
ourselves and our Posterity, do ordain and establish this
Constitution for the United States of America.

Article. I.

SECTION. 1.

All legislative Powers herein granted shall be vested in a Congress of the United
States, which shall consist of a Senate and House of Representatives.

SECTION. 2.

The House of Representatives shall be composed of Members chosen every second
Year by the People of the several States, and the Electors in each State shall have
the Qualifications requisite for Electors of the most numerous Branch of the State
Legislature.

No Person shall be a Representative who shall not have attained to the Age of
twenty five Years, and been seven Years a Citizen of the United States, and who
shall not, when elected, be an Inhabitant of that State in which he shall be chosen.

[Representatives and direct Taxes shall be apportioned among the several States
which may be included within this Union, according to their respective Numbers,
which shall be determined by adding to the whole Number of free Persons,
including those bound to Service for a Term of Years, and excluding Indians not
taxed, three fifths of all other Persons.]* The actual Enumeration shall be made
within three Years after the first Meeting of the Congress of the United States,
and within every subsequent Term of ten Years, in such Manner as they shall
by Law direct. The Number of Representatives shall not exceed one for every
thirty Thousand, but each State shall have at Least one Representative; and until
such enumeration shall be made, the State of New Hampshire shall be entitled to

chuse three, Massachusetts eight, Rhode-Island and Providence Plantations one, Connecticut five, New-York six, New Jersey four, Pennsylvania eight, Delaware one, Maryland six, Virginia ten, North Carolina five, South Carolina five, and Georgia three.

When vacancies happen in the Representation from any State, the Executive Authority thereof shall issue Writs of Election to fill such Vacancies.

The House of Representatives shall chuse their Speaker and other Officers; and shall have the sole Power of Impeachment.

SECTION. 3.

The Senate of the United States shall be composed of two Senators from each State, [chosen by the Legislature thereof,]* for six Years; and each Senator shall have one Vote.

Immediately after they shall be assembled in Consequence of the first Election, they shall be divided as equally as may be into three Classes. The Seats of the Senators of the first Class shall be vacated at the Expiration of the second Year, of the second Class at the Expiration of the fourth Year, and of the third Class at the Expiration of the sixth Year, so that one third may be chosen every second Year; [and if Vacancies happen by Resignation, or otherwise, during the Recess of the Legislature of any State, the Executive thereof may make temporary Appointments until the next Meeting of the Legislature, which shall then fill such Vacancies.]*

No Person shall be a Senator who shall not have attained to the Age of thirty Years, and been nine Years a Citizen of the United States, and who shall not, when elected, be an Inhabitant of that State for which he shall be chosen.

The Vice President of the United States shall be
President of the Senate, but shall have no Vote, unless they be equally divided.

The Senate shall chuse their other Officers, and also a President pro tempore, in the Absence of the Vice President, or when he shall exercise the Office of President of the United States.

The Senate shall have the sole Power to try all Impeachments. When sitting for that Purpose, they shall be on Oath or Affirmation. When the President of the United States is tried, the Chief Justice shall preside: And no Person shall be convicted without the Concurrence of two thirds of the Members present.

Judgment in Cases of Impeachment shall not extend further than to removal from Office, and disqualification to hold and enjoy any Office of honor, Trust or Profit under the United States: but the Party convicted shall nevertheless be liable and subject to Indictment, Trial, Judgment and Punishment, according to Law.

SECTION. 4.

The Times, Places and Manner of holding Elections for Senators and Representatives, shall be prescribed in each State by the Legislature thereof; but the Congress may at any time by Law make or alter such Regulations, except as to the Places of chusing Senators.

The Congress shall assemble at least once in every Year, and such Meeting shall be [on the first Monday in December,]* unless they shall by Law appoint a different Day.

SECTION. 5.

Each House shall be the Judge of the Elections, Returns and Qualifications of its own Members, and a Majority of each shall constitute a Quorum to do Business; but a smaller Number may adjourn from day to day, and may be authorized to compel the Attendance of absent Members, in such Manner, and under such Penalties as each House may provide.

Each House may determine the Rules of its Proceedings, punish its Members for disorderly Behaviour, and, with the Concurrence of two thirds, expel a Member. Each House shall keep a Journal of its Proceedings, and from time to time publish the same, excepting such Parts as may in their Judgment require Secrecy; and the Yeas and Nays of the Members of either House on any question shall, at the Desire of one fifth of those Present, be entered on the Journal.

Neither House, during the Session of Congress, shall, without the Consent of the other, adjourn for more than three days, nor to any other Place than that in which the two Houses shall be sitting.

SECTION. 6.

The Senators and Representatives shall receive a Compensation for their Services, to be ascertained by Law, and paid out of the Treasury of the United States. They shall in all
Cases, except Treason, Felony and Breach of the Peace, be privileged from Arrest during their Attendance at the Session of their respective Houses, and in going to and returning from the same; and for any Speech or Debate in either House, they shall not be questioned in any other Place.

No Senator or Representative shall, during the Time for which he was elected, be appointed to any civil Office under the Authority of the United States, which shall have been created, or the Emoluments whereof shall have been increased during such time; and no Person holding any Office under the United States, shall be a Member of either House during his Continuance in Office.

SECTION. 7.

All Bills for raising Revenue shall originate in the House of Representatives; but the Senate may propose or concur with Amendments as on other Bills.

Every Bill which shall have passed the House of Representatives and the Senate, shall, before it become a Law, be presented to the President of the United States; If he approve he shall sign it, but if not he shall return it, with his Objections to that House in which it shall have originated, who shall enter the Objections at large on their Journal, and proceed to reconsider it. If after such Reconsideration two thirds of that House shall agree to pass the Bill, it shall be sent, together with the Objections, to the other House, by which it shall likewise be reconsidered, and if approved by two thirds of that House, it shall become a Law. But in all such Cases the Votes of both Houses shall be determined by Yeas and Nays, and the Names of the Persons voting for and against the Bill shall be entered on the Journal of each House respectively, If any Bill shall not be returned by the President within ten Days (Sundays excepted) after it shall have been presented to him, the Same shall be a Law, in like Manner as if he had signed it, unless the Congress by their Adjournament prevent its Return, in which Case it shall not be a Law.

Every Order, Resolution, or Vote to which the Concurrence of the Senate and House of Representatives may be necessary (except on a question of Adjournment) shall be presented to the President of the United States; and before the Same shall take Effect, shall be approved by him, or being disapproved by him, shall be repassed by two thirds of the Senate and House of Representatives, according to the Rules and Limitations prescribed in the Case of a Bill.

SECTION. 8.

The Congress shall have Power To lay and collect Taxes, Duties, Imposts and Excises, to pay the Debts and provide for the common Defence and general Welfare of the United States; but all Duties, Imposts and Excises shall be uniform throughout the United States;

To borrow Money on the credit of the United States;

To regulate Commerce with foreign Nations, and among the several States, and with the Indian Tribes;

To establish an uniform Rule of Naturalization, and uniform Laws on the subject of Bankruptcies throughout the United States;

To coin Money, regulate the Value thereof, and of foreign Coin, and fix the Standard of Weights and Measures;

To provide for the Punishment of counterfeiting the Securities and current Coin of the United States; To establish Post Offices and post Roads;

To promote the Progress of Science and useful Arts, by securing for limited Times to Authors and Inventors the exclusive Right to their respective Writings and Discoveries;

To constitute Tribunals inferior to the supreme Court;

To define and punish Piracies and Felonies committed on the high Seas, and Offenses against the Law of Nations;

To declare War, grant Letters of Marque and Reprisal, and make Rules concerning Captures on Land and Water;

To raise and support Armies, but no Appropriation of Money to that Use shall be for a longer Term than two Years;

To provide and maintain a Navy;

To make Rules for the Government and Regulation of the land and naval Forces;

To provide for calling forth the Militia to execute the Laws of the Union, suppress Insurrections and repel Invasions;

To provide for organizing, arming, and disciplining, the Militia, and for governing such Part of them as may be employed in the Service of the United States, reserving to the States respectively, the Appointment of the Officers, and the Authority of training the Militia according to the discipline prescribed by Congress;

To exercise exclusive Legislation in all Cases whatsoever, over such District (not exceeding ten Miles square) as may, by Cession of particular States, and the Acceptance of Congress, become the Seat of the Government of the United States, and to exercise like Authority over all Places purchased by the Consent of the Legislature of the State in which the Same shall be, for the Erection of Forts, Magazines, Arsenals, dock-Yards and other needful Buildings;
-And

To make all Laws which shall be necessary and proper for carrying into Execution the foregoing Powers, and all other Powers vested by this Constitution in the Government of the United States, or in any Department or Officer thereof.

SECTION. 9.

The Migration or Importation of such Persons as any of the States now existing shall think proper to admit, shall not be prohibited by the Congress prior to the Year one thousand eight hundred and eight, but a Tax or duty may be imposed on such Importation, not exceeding ten dollars for each Person.

The Privilege of the Writ of Habeas Corpus shall not be suspended, unless when in Cases of Rebellion or Invasion the public Safety may require it.

No Bill of Attainder or ex post facto Law shall be passed.

[No Capitation, or other direct, Tax shall be laid, unless in Proportion to the Census or Enumeration herein before directed to be taken.]*

No Tax or Duty shall be laid on Articles exported from any State.

No Preference shall be given by any Regulation of Commerce or Revenue to the Ports of one State over those of another: nor shall Vessels bound to, or from, one State, be obliged to enter, clear, or pay Duties in another.

No Money shall be drawn from the Treasury, but in Consequence of Appropriations made by Law; and a regular Statement and Account of the Receipts and Expenditures of all public Money shall be published from time to time.

No Title of Nobility shall be granted by the United States: And no Person holding any Office of Profit or Trust under them, shall, without the Consent of the Congress, accept of any present, Emolument, Office, or Title, of any kind whatever, from any King, Prince, or foreign State.

Article. II.

SECTION. 1.

The executive Power shall be vested in a President of the United States of America. He shall hold his Office during the Term of four Years, and, together with the Vice President, chosen for the same Term, be elected, as follows:

Each State shall appoint, in such Manner as the Legislature thereof may direct, a Number of Electors, equal to the whole Number of Senators and Representatives to which the State may be entitled in the Congress: but no Senator or Representative, or Person holding an Office of Trust or Profit under the United States, shall be appointed an Elector.

[The Electors shall meet in their respective States, and vote by Ballot for two Persons, of whom one at least shall not be an Inhabitant of the same State with themselves. And they shall make a List of all the Persons voted for, and of the Number of Votes for each; which List they shall sign and certify, and transmit sealed to the Seat of the Government of the United States, directed to the President of the Senate. The President of the Senate shall, in the Presence of the Senate and House of Representatives, open all the Certificates, and the Votes shall then be counted. The Person having the greatest Number of Votes shall be the President, if such Number be a Majority of the whole Number of Electors appointed; and if there be more than one who have such Majority, and have an equal Number of Votes, then the House of Representatives shall immediately chuse by Ballot one of them for President; and if no Person have a Majority, then from the fi ve highest on the List the said House shall in like Manner chuse the President. But in chusing the President, the Votes shall be taken by States, the Representation from each State having one Vote; A quorum for this Purpose shall consist of a Member or Members from two thirds of the States, and a Majority of all the States shall be necessary to a Choice. In every Case, after the Choice of the President, the Person having the greatest Number of Votes of the Electors shall be the Vice President. But if there should remain two or more who have equal Votes, the Senate shall chuse from them by Ballot the Vice President.]*

The Congress may determine the Time of chusing the Electors, and the Day on which they shall give their Votes; which Day shall be the same throughout the United States.

No Person except a natural born Citizen, or a Citizen of the United States, at the time of the Adoption of this Constitution, shall be eligible to the Office of President; neither shall any person be eligible to that Office who shall not have attained to the Age of thirty five Years, and been fourteen Years a Resident within the United States.

[In Case of the Removal of the President from Office, or of his Death, Resignation, or Inability to discharge the Powers and Duties of the said Office, the Same shall devolve on the Vice President, and the Congress may by Law provide for the Case of Removal, Death, Resignation or Inability, both of the President and Vice President, declaring what Officer shall then act as President, and such Officer shall act accordingly, until the Disability be removed, or a President shall be elected.]*

The President shall, at stated Times, receive for his Services, a Compensation, which shall neither be increased nor diminished during the Period for which he shall have been elected, and he shall not receive within that Period any other Emolument from the United States, or any of them.

Before he enter on the Execution of his Office, he shall take the following Oath or Affirmation:—"I do solemnly swear (or affirm) that I will faithfully execute the Office of President of the United States, and will to the best of my Ability, preserve, protect and defend the Constitution of the United States."

SECTION. 2.

The President shall be Commander in Chief of the Army and Navy of the United States, and of the Militia of the several States, when called into the actual Service of the United States; he may require the Opinion, in writing, of the principal Officer in each of the executive Departments, upon any Subject relating to the Duties of their respective Offices, and he shall have Power to grant Reprieves and Pardons for Offenses against the United States, except in Cases of Impeachment.

He shall have Power, by and with the Advice and Consent of the Senate, to make Treaties, provided two thirds of the Senators present concur; and he shall nominate, and by and with the Advice and Consent of the Senate, shall appoint Ambassadors, other public Ministers and Consuls, Judges of the supreme Court, and all other Officers of the United States, whose Appointments are not herein otherwise provided for, and which shall be established by Law: but the Congress may by Law vest the Appointment of such inferior Officers, as they think proper, in the President alone, in the Courts of Law, or in the Heads of Departments.

The President shall have Power to fill up all Vacancies that may happen during the Recess of the Senate, by granting Commissions which shall expire at the End of their next Session.

SECTION. 3.

He shall from time to time give to the Congress Information of the State of the Union, and recommend to their Consideration such Measures as he shall judge necessary and expedient; he may, on extraordinary Occasions, convene both Houses, or either of them, and in Case of Disagreement between them, with Respect to the Time of Adjournment, he may adjourn them to such Time as he shall think proper; he shall receive Ambassadors and other public Ministers; he shall take Care that the Laws be faithfully executed, and shall Commission all the Officers of the United States.

SECTION. 4.

The President, Vice President and all civil Officers of the United States, shall be removed from Office on Impeachment for, and Conviction of, Treason, Bribery, or other high Crimes and Misdemeanors.

Article. III.

SECTION. 1.

The judicial Power of the United States, shall be vested in one supreme Court, and in such inferior Courts as the Congress may from time to time ordain and establish. The Judges, both of the supreme and inferior Courts, shall hold their Offices during good Behaviour, and shall at stated Times, receive for their Services, a Compensation, which shall not be diminished during their Continuance in Office.

SECTION. 2.

The judicial Power shall extend to all Cases, in Law and Equity, arising under this Constitution, the Laws of the United States, and Treaties made, or which shall be made, under their Authority;—to all Cases affecting Ambassadors, other public Ministers and Consuls;—to all Cases of admiralty and maritime Jurisdiction;—to Controversies to which the United States shall be a Party;—to Controversies between two or more States;—[between a State and Citizens of another State;-]* between Citizens of different States,—between Citizens of the same State claiming Lands under Grants of different States, [and between a State, or the Citizens thereof;—and foreign States, Citizens or Subjects.]*

In all Cases affecting Ambassadors, other public Ministers and Consuls, and those in which a State shall be Party, the supreme Court shall have original Jurisdiction. In all the other Cases before mentioned, the supreme Court shall have appellate Jurisdiction, both as to Law and Fact, with such Exceptions, and under such Regulations as the Congress shall make.

The Trial of all Crimes, except in Cases of Impeachment; shall be by Jury; and such Trial shall be held in the State where the said Crimes shall have been committed; but when not committed within any State, the Trial shall be at such Place or Places as the Congress may by Law have directed.

SECTION. 3.

Treason against the United States, shall consist only in levying War against them, or in adhering to their Enemies, giving them Aid and Comfort. No Person shall be convicted of Treason unless on the Testimony of two Witnesses to the same overt Act, or on Confession in open Court.

The Congress shall have Power to declare the Punishment of Treason, but no Attainder of Treason shall work Corruption of Blood, or Forfeiture except during the Life of the Person attainted.

Article. IV.

SECTION. 1.

Full Faith and Credit shall be given in each State to the public Acts, Records, and judicial Proceedings of every other State. And the Congress may by general Laws prescribe the Manner in which such Acts, Records and Proceedings shall be proved, and the Effect thereof.

SECTION. 2.

The Citizens of each State shall be entitled to all Privileges and Immunities of Citizens in the several States.

A Person charged in any State with Treason, Felony, or other Crime, who shall flee from Justice, and be found in another State, shall on Demand of the executive Authority of the State from which he fled, be delivered up, to be removed to the State having Jurisdiction of the Crime.

[No Person held to Service or Labour in one State, under the Laws thereof, escaping into another, shall, in Consequence of any Law or Regulation therein, be discharged from such Service or Labour, but shall be delivered up on Claim of the Party to whom such Service or Labour may be due.]*

SECTION. 3.

New States may be admitted by the Congress into this Union; but no new State shall be formed or erected within the Jurisdiction of any other State; nor any State be formed by the Junction of two or more States, or Parts of States, without the Consent of the Legislatures of the States concerned as well as of the Congress.

The Congress shall have Power to dispose of and make all needful Rules and Regulations respecting the Territory or other Property belonging to the United States; and nothing in this Constitution shall be so construed as to Prejudice any Claims of the United States, or of any particular State.

SECTION. 4.

The United States shall guarantee to every State in this Union a Republican Form of Government, and shall protect each of them against Invasion; and on Application of the Legislature, or of the Executive (when the Legislature cannot be convened) against domestic Violence.

Article. V.

The Congress, whenever two thirds of both Houses shall deem it necessary, shall propose Amendments to this Constitution, or, on the Application of the Legislatures of two thirds of the several States, shall call a Convention for proposing Amendments, which in either Case, shall be valid to all Intents and Purposes, as Part of this Constitution, when ratified by the Legislatures of three-fourths of the several States, or by Conventions in three fourths thereof, as the one or the other Mode of Ratifi cation may be proposed by the Congress; Provided that no Amendment which may be made prior to the Year One thousand eight hundred and eight shall in any Manner affect the first and fourth Clauses in the Ninth Section of the first Article; and that no State, without its Consent, shall be deprived of its equal Suffrage in the Senate.

Article. VI.

All Debts contracted and Engagements entered into, before the Adoption of this Constitution, shall be as valid against the United States under this Constitution, as under the Confederation.

This Constitution, and the Laws of the United States which shall be made in Pursuance thereof; and all Treaties made, or which shall be made, under the Authority of the United States, shall be the supreme Law of the Land; and the Judges in every State shall be bound thereby, any Thing in the Constitution or Laws of any State to the Contrary notwithstanding.

The Senators and Representatives before mentioned, and the Members of the several State Legislatures, and all executive and judicial Officers, both of the United States and of the several States, shall be bound by Oath or Affirmation, to support this Constitution; but no religious Test shall ever be required as a Qualification to any Office or public Trust under the United States.

Article. VII.

The Ratification of the Conventions of nine States, shall be sufficient for the Establishment of this Constitution between the States so ratifying the Same.

Done in Convention by the Unanimous Consent of the States present the Seventeenth Day of September in the Year of our Lord one thousand seven hundred and Eighty seven and of the Independence of the United States of America the Twelfth In Witness whereof We have hereunto subscribed our Names,

Go. Washington—Presidt: and deputy from Virginia

NEW HAMPSHIRE

    John Langdon
    Nicholas Gilman

MASSACHUSETTS

    Nathaniel Gorham
    Rufus King

CONNECTICUT

    Wm. Saml. Johnson
    Roger Sherman

NEW YORK

    Alexander Hamilton

NEW JERSEY

Wil: Livingston
David Brearley
Wm. Paterson
Jona: Dayton

PENNSYLVANIA

B Franklin
Thomas Miffl in
Robt Morris
Geo. Clymer
Thos. FitzSimons
Jared Ingersoll
James Wilson
Gouv Morris

DELAWARE

Geo: Read
Gunning Bedford jun
John Dickinson
Richard Bassett
Jaco: Broom

MARYLAND

James McHenry
Dan of St. Thos. Jenifer
Danl Carroll

VIRGINIA

John Blair-
James Madison Jr.

NORTH CAROLINA

Wm. Blount
Richd. Dobbs Spaight
Hu Williamson

SOUTH CAROLINA

J. Rutledge
Charles Cotesworth Pinckney
Charles Pinckney
Pierce Butler

GEORGIA

William Few
Abr Baldwin

Attest William Jackson Secretary
In Convention Monday
September 17th, 1787.
Present
The States of
New Hampshire, Massachusetts, Connecticut, Mr. Hamilton from New York, New Jersey, Pennsylvania, Delaware, Maryland, Virginia, North Carolina, South Carolina and
Georgia.

Resolved,
That the preceeding Constitution be laid before the United States in Congress assembled, and that it is the Opinion of this Convention, that it should afterwards be submitted to a Convention of Delegates, chosen in each State by the People thereof, under the Recommendation of its Legislature, for their Assent and Ratification; and that each Convention assenting to, and ratifying the Same, should give Notice thereof to the United States in Congress assembled. Resolved, That it is the Opinion of this Convention, that as soon as the Conventions of nine States shall have ratified this Constitution, the United States in Congress assembled should fix a Day on which Electors should be appointed by the States which shall

have ratified the same, and a Day on which the Electors should assemble to vote for the President, and the Time and Place for commencing Proceedings under this Constitution.

That after such Publication the Electors should be appointed, and the Senators and Representatives elected: That the Electors should meet on the Day fixed for the Election of the President, and should transmit their Votes certified, signed, sealed and directed, as the Constitution requires, to the Secretary of the United States in Congress assembled, that the Senators and Representatives should convene at the Time and Place assigned; that the Senators should appoint a President of the Senate, for the sole Purpose of receiving, opening and counting the Votes for President; and, that after he shall be chosen, the Congress, together with the President, should, without Delay, proceed to execute this Constitution.

By the unanimous Order of the Convention

Go. Washington-Presidt:
W. JACKSON Secretary.

* Language in brackets has been changed by amendment.

THE AMENDMENTS TO THE CONSTITUTION OF THE UNITED STATES AS RATIFIED BY THE STATES

Preamble to the
Bill of Rights

Congress of the United States
begun and held at the City of New-York, on
Wednesday the fourth of March,
one thousand seven hundred and eighty nine

THE Conventions of a number of the States, having at the time of their adopting the Constitution, expressed a desire, in order to prevent misconstruction or abuse of its powers, that further declaratory and restrictive clauses should be added: And as extending the ground of public confidence in the Government, will best ensure the beneficent ends of its institution.

RESOLVED by the Senate and House of Representatives of the United States of America, in Congress assembled, two thirds of both Houses concurring, that the following Articles be proposed to the Legislatures of the several States, as amendments to the Constitution of the United States, all, or any of which Articles, when ratified by three fourths of the said Legislatures, to be valid to all intents and purposes, as part of the said Constitution; viz.

ARTICLES in addition to, and Amendment of the Constitution of the United States of America, proposed by Congress, and ratified by the Legislatures of the several States, pursuant to the fifth Article of the original Constitution.

(Note: The first 10 amendments to the Constitution were ratified December 15, 1791, and form what is known as the "Bill of Rights.")

Amendment I.

Congress shall make no law respecting an establishment of religion, or prohibiting the free exercise thereof; or abridging the freedom of speech, or of the press, or the right of the people peaceably to assemble, and to petition the Government for a redress of grievances.

Amendment II.

A well regulated Militia, being necessary to the security of a free State, the right of the people to keep and bear Arms, shall not be infringed.

Amendment III.

No Soldier shall, in time of peace be quartered in any house, without the consent of the Owner, nor in time of war, but in a manner to be prescribed by law.

Amendment IV.

The right of the people to be secure in their persons, houses, papers, and effects, against unreasonable searches and seizures, shall not be violated, and no Warrants shall issue, but upon probable cause, supported by Oath or affirmation, and particularly describing the place to be searched, and the persons or things to be seized.

Amendment V.

No person shall be held to answer for a capital, or otherwise infamous crime, unless on a presentment or indictment of a Grand Jury, except in cases arising in the land or naval forces, or in the Militia, when in actual service in time of War or public danger; nor shall any person be subject for the same offence to be twice put in jeopardy of life or limb; nor shall be compelled in any criminal case to be a witness against himself, nor be deprived of life, liberty, or property, without due process of law; nor shall private property be taken for public use, without just compensation.

Amendment VI.

In all criminal prosecutions, the accused shall enjoy the right to a speedy and public trial, by an impartial jury of the State and district wherein the crime shall have been committed, which district shall have been previously ascertained by law, and to be informed of the nature and cause of the accusation; to be confronted with the witnesses against him; to have compulsory process for obtaining witnesses in his favor, and to have the Assistance of Counsel for his defence.

Amendment VII.

In suits at common law, where the value in controversy shall exceed twenty dollars, the right of trial by jury shall be preserved, and no fact tried by a jury shall be otherwise reexamined in any Court of the United States, than according to the rules of the common law.

Amendment VIII.

Excessive bail shall not be required, nor excessive fines imposed, nor cruel and unusual punishments inflicted.

Amendment IX.

The enumeration in the Constitution, of certain rights, shall not be construed to deny or disparage others retained by the people.

Amendment X.

The powers not delegated to the United States by the Constitution, nor prohibited by it to the States, are reserved to the States respectively, or to the people.

AMENDMENTS 11-27

Amendment XI.

Passed by Congress March 4, 1794. Ratified February 7, 1795.

(Note: A portion of Article III, Section 2 of the Constitution was modified by the 11th Amendment.)

The Judicial power of the United States shall not be construed to extend to any suit in law or equity, commenced or prosecuted against one of the United States by Citizens of another State, or by Citizens or Subjects of any Foreign State.

Amendment XII.

Passed by Congress December 9, 1803. Ratified June 15, 1804.

(Note: A portion of Article II, Section 1 of the Constitution was changed by the 12th Amendment.)

The Electors shall meet in their respective states, and vote by ballot for President and Vice President, one of whom, at least, shall not be an inhabitant of the same state with themselves; they shall name in their ballots the person voted for as President, and in distinct ballots the person voted for as Vice-President, and they shall make distinct lists of all persons voted for as President, and of all persons voted for as Vice-President, and of the number of votes for each, which lists they shall sign and certify, and transmit sealed to the seat of the government of the United States, directed to the President of the Senate;-the President of the Senate shall, in the presence of the Senate and House of Representatives, open all the certificates and the votes shall then be counted;-The person having the greatest number of votes for President, shall be the President, if such number be a majority of the whole number of Electors appointed; and if no person have such majority, then from the persons having the highest numbers not exceeding three on the list of those voted for as President, the House of Representatives shall choose immediately, by ballot, the President. But in choosing the President, the votes shall be taken by states, the representation from each state having one vote; a quorum for this purpose shall consist of a member or members from two-thirds of the states, and a majority of all the states shall be necessary to a choice. [And if the House of Representatives shall not choose a President whenever the right of choice shall devolve upon them, before the fourth day of March next following, then the Vice-President shall act as President, as in case of the death or other constitutional disability of the President.-]* The person having the greatest number of votes as Vice-President, shall be the Vice-President, if such number be a majority of the whole number of Electors appointed, and if no person have a majority, then from the two highest numbers on the list, the Senate shall choose the Vice President; a quorum for the purpose shall consist of two-thirds of the whole number of Senators, and a majority of the whole number shall be necessary to a choice. But no person constitutionally ineligible to the office of President shall be eligible to that of Vice President of the United States.

*Superseded by Section 3 of the 20th Amendment.

Amendment XIII.

Passed by Congress January 31, 1865. Ratified December 6, 1865.

(Note: A portion of Article IV, Section 2 of the Constitution was changed by the 13th Amendment.)

SECTION 1.

Neither slavery nor involuntary servitude, except as a punishment for crime whereof the party shall have been duly convicted, shall exist within the United States, or any place subject to their jurisdiction.

SECTION 2.

Congress shall have power to enforce this article by appropriate legislation.

Amendment XIV.

Passed by Congress June 13, 1866. Ratified July 9, 1868.

(Note: Article I, Section 2 of the Constitution was modified by Section 2 of the 14th Amendment.)

SECTION 1.

All persons born or naturalized in the United States and subject to the jurisdiction thereof, are citizens of the United States and of the State wherein they reside. No State shall make or enforce any law which shall abridge the privileges or immunities of citizens of the United States; nor shall any State deprive any person of life, liberty, or property, without due process of law; nor deny to any person within its jurisdiction the equal protection of the laws.

SECTION 2.

Representatives shall be apportioned among the several States according to their respective numbers, counting the whole number of persons in each State, excluding Indians not taxed. But when the right to vote at any election for the choice of electors for President and Vice President of the United States, Representatives in Congress, the Executive and Judicial officers of a State, or the members of the Legislature thereof, is denied to any of the male inhabitants of such State, [being twenty-one years of age,]* and citizens of the United States, or in any way abridged, except for participation in rebellion, or other crime, the basis of representation therein shall be reduced in the proportion which the number of such male citizens shall bear to the whole number of male citizens twenty-one years of age in such State.

SECTION 3.

No person shall be a Senator or Representative in Congress, or elector of President and Vice President, or hold any office, civil or military, under the United States, or under any State, who, having previously taken an oath, as a member of Congress, or as an officer of the United States, or as a member of any State legislature, or as an executive or judicial officer of any State, to support the Constitution of the United States, shall have engaged in insurrection or rebellion against the same, or given aid or comfort to the enemies thereof. But Congress may by a vote of two-thirds of each House, remove such disability.

SECTION 4.

The validity of the public debt of the United States, authorized by law, including debts incurred for payment of pensions and bounties for services in suppressing insurrection or rebellion, shall not be questioned. But neither the United States nor any State shall assume or pay any debt or obligation incurred in aid of insurrection or rebellion against the United States, or any claim for the loss or emancipation of any slave; but all such debts, obligations and claims shall be held illegal and void.

SECTION 5.

The Congress shall have the power to enforce, by appropriate legislation, the provisions of this article.

*Changed by Section 1 of the 26th Amendment.

Amendment XV.

Passed by Congress February 26, 1869. Ratified February 3, 1870.

SECTION 1.

The right of citizens of the United States to vote shall not be denied or abridged by the United States or by any State on account of race, color, or previous condition of servitude.

SECTION 2.

The Congress shall have the power to enforce this article by appropriate legislation.

Amendment XVI.

Passed by Congress July 2, 1909. Ratified February 3, 1913.

(Note: Article I, Section 9 of the Constitution was modified by the 16th Amendment.) The Congress shall have power to lay and collect taxes on incomes, from whatever source derived, without apportionment among the several States, and without regard to any census or enumeration.

Amendment XVII.

Passed by Congress May 13, 1912. Ratified April 8, 1913.

(Note: Article I, Section 3 of the Constitution was modified by the 17th Amendment.)

The Senate of the United States shall be composed of two Senators from each State, elected by the people thereof, for six years; and each Senator shall have one vote. The electors in each State shall have the qualifications requisite for electors of the most numerous branch of the State legislatures.

When vacancies happen in the representation of any State in the Senate, the executive authority of such State shall issue writs of election to fill such vacancies: Provided, That the legislature of any State may empower the executive thereof to make temporary appointments until the people fill the vacancies by election as the legislature may direct.

This amendment shall not be so construed as to affect the election or term of any Senator chosen before it becomes valid as part of the Constitution.

Amendment XVIII.

Passed by Congress December 18, 1917. Ratified January 16, 1919. Repealed by the 21st Amendment, December 5, 1933.

SECTION 1.

After one year from the ratification of this article the manufacture, sale, or transportation of intoxicating liquors within, the importation thereof into, or the exportation thereof from the United States and all territory subject to the jurisdiction thereof for beverage purposes is hereby prohibited.

SECTION 2.

The Congress and the several States shall have concurrent power to enforce this article by appropriate legislation.

SECTION 3.

This article shall be inoperative unless it shall have been ratified as an amendment to the Constitution by the legislatures of the several States, as provided in the Constitution, within seven years from the date of the submission hereof to the States by the Congress.

Amendment XIX.

Passed by Congress June 4, 1919. Ratified August 18, 1920.

The right of citizens of the United States to vote shall not be denied or abridged by the United States or by any State on account of sex.

Congress shall have power to enforce this article by appropriate legislation.

Amendment XX.

Passed by Congress March 2, 1932. Ratified January 23, 1933.

(Note: Article I, Section 4 of the Constitution was modified by Section 2 of this Amendment. In addition, a portion of the 12th Amendment was superseded by Section 3.)

SECTION 1.

The terms of the President and the Vice President shall end at noon on the 20th day of January, and the terms of Senators and Representatives at noon on the 3d day of January, of the years in which such terms would have ended if this article had not been ratified; and the terms of their successors shall then begin.

SECTION 2.

The Congress shall assemble at least once in every year, and such meeting shall begin at noon on the 3d day of January, unless they shall by law appoint a different day.

SECTION 3.

If, at the time fixed for the beginning of the term of the President, the President elect shall have died, the Vice President elect shall become President. If a President shall not have been chosen before the time fixed for the beginning of his term, or if the President elect shall have failed to qualify, then the Vice President elect shall act as President until a President shall have qualified; and the Congress may by law provide for the case wherein neither a President elect nor a Vice President shall have qualified, declaring who shall then act as President, or the manner in which one who is to act shall be selected, and such person shall act accordingly until a President or Vice President shall have qualified.

SECTION 4.

The Congress may by law provide for the case of the death of any of the persons from whom the House of Representatives may choose a President whenever the right of choice shall have devolved upon them, and for the case of the death of any of the persons from whom the Senate may choose a Vice President whenever the right of choice shall have devolved upon them.

SECTION 5.

Sections 1 and 2 shall take effect on the 15th day of October following the ratification of this article.

SECTION 6.

This article shall be inoperative unless it shall have been ratified as an amendment to the Constitution by the legislatures of three-fourths of the several States within seven years from the date of its submission.

Amendment XXI.

Passed by Congress February 20, 1933. Ratified December 5, 1933.

SECTION 1.

The eighteenth article of amendment to the Constitution of the United States is hereby repealed.

SECTION 2.

The transportation or importation into any State, Territory, or possession of the United States for delivery or use therein of intoxicating liquors, in violation of the laws thereof, is hereby prohibited.

SECTION 3.

This article shall be inoperative unless it shall have been ratified as an amendment to the Constitution by conventions in the several States, as provided in the Constitution, within seven years from the date of the submission hereof to the States by the Congress.

Amendment XXII.

Passed by Congress March 21, 1947. Ratified February 27, 1951.

SECTION 1.

No person shall be elected to the office of the President more than twice, and no person who has held the office of President, or acted as President, for more than two years of a term to which some other person was elected President shall be elected to the office of President more than once. But this Article shall not apply to any person holding the office of President when this Article was proposed by Congress, and shall not prevent any person who may be holding the office of President, or acting as President, during the term within which this Article becomes operative from holding the office of President or acting as President during the remainder of such term.

SECTION 2.

This article shall be inoperative unless it shall have been ratified as an amendment to the Constitution by the legislatures of three-fourths of the several States within seven years from the date of its submission to the States by the Congress.

Amendment XXIII.

Passed by Congress June 16, 1960. Ratified March 29, 1961.

SECTION 1.

The District constituting the seat of Government of the United States shall appoint in such manner as Congress may direct:

A number of electors of President and Vice President equal to the whole number of Senators and Representatives in Congress to which the District would be entitled if it were a State, but in no event more than the least populous State; they shall be in addition to those appointed by the States, but they shall be considered, for the purposes of the election of President and Vice President, to be electors appointed by a State; and they shall meet in the District and perform such duties as provided by the twelfth article of amendment.

SECTION 2.

The Congress shall have power to enforce this article by appropriate legislation.

Amendment XXIV.

Passed by Congress August 27, 1962. Ratified January 23, 1964.

SECTION 1.

The right of citizens of the United States to vote in any primary or other election for President or Vice President, for electors for President or Vice President, or for Senator or Representative in Congress, shall not be denied or abridged by the United States or any State by reason of failure to pay poll tax or other tax.

SECTION 2.

The Congress shall have power to enforce this article by appropriate legislation.

Amendment XXV.

Passed by Congress July 6, 1965. Ratified February 10, 1967.

(Note: Article II, Section 1 of the Constitution was modified by the 25th Amendment.)

SECTION 1.

In case of the removal of the President from office or of his death or resignation, the Vice President shall become President.

SECTION 2.

Whenever there is a vacancy in the office of the Vice President, the President shall nominate a Vice President who shall take office upon confirmation by a majority vote of both Houses of Congress.

SECTION 3.

Whenever the President transmits to the President pro tempore of the Senate and the Speaker of the House of Representatives his written declaration that he is unable to discharge the powers and duties of his office, and until he transmits to them a written declaration to the contrary, such powers and duties shall be discharged by the Vice President as Acting President.

SECTION 4.

Whenever the Vice President and a majority of either the principal officers of the executive departments or of such other body as Congress may by law provide, transmit to the President pro tempore of the Senate and the Speaker of the House of Representatives their written declaration that the President is unable to discharge the powers and duties of his office, the Vice President shall immediately assume the powers and duties of the office as Acting President.

Thereafter, when the President transmits to the President pro tempore of the Senate and the Speaker of the House of Representatives his written declaration that no inability exists, he shall resume the powers and duties of his office unless the Vice President and a majority of either the principal officers of the executive department or of such other body as Congress may by law provide, transmit within four days to the President pro tempore of the Senate and the Speaker of the House of Representatives their written declaration that the President is unable to discharge the powers and duties of his office.

Thereupon Congress shall decide the issue, assembling within forty-eight hours for that purpose if not in session. If the Congress, within twenty-one days after receipt of the latter written declaration, or, if Congress is not in session, within twenty-one days after Congress is required to assemble, determines by two-thirds vote of both Houses that the President is unable to discharge the powers and duties of his office, the Vice President shall continue to discharge the same as Acting President; otherwise, the President shall resume the powers and duties of his office.

Amendment XXVI.

Passed by Congress March 23, 1971. Ratified July 1, 1971.

(Note: Amendment 14, Section 2 of the Constitution was modified by Section 1 of the 26th Amendment.)

SECTION 1.

The right of citizens of the United States, who are eighteen years of age or older, to vote shall not be denied or abridged by the United States or by any State on account of age.

SECTION 2.

The Congress shall have power to enforce this article by appropriate legislation.

Amendment XXVII.

Originally proposed Sept. 25, 1789. Ratified May 7, 1992.

No law, varying the compensation for the services of the Senators and Representatives, shall take effect, until an election of representatives shall have intervened.

The NCC is an independent, non-partisan, nonprofit organization that was established in 1988 under the Constitution Heritage Act. The Center's mission is to increase awareness and understanding of the Constitution, the Constitution's history and its relevance to people's daily lives.
National Constitution Center
525 Arch Street
Independence Mall
Philadelphia, PA 19106
(215) 409-6600
www.constitutioncenter.org

AUTHORS PAGE

Eugene Chiaverini has dedicated his professional life to working in the field of human services, providing counseling to children and adults. He began his career in 1963, after graduating from Muskingum College with a major in Psychology and History. He earned his Master in Social Work from Case-Western Reserve University. Mr. Chiaverini worked in a variety of private and public organizations as a clinician, administrator and clinical director. In addition, he has served as a consultant in nursing homes, worked with learning-disabled children in special schools and had a successful private practice

Mr. Chiaverini has immersed himself in studying holistic treatment models, Eastern healing practices and the value of integrating both models in assisting his clients heal in mind, body and spirit

In 2006, Mr. Chiaverini served as a delegate to China for the US-China Conference on Social Work. He is listed in Cambridge "Who's Who" registry of Executives and Professional. He retired in 2007.